W9-DFD-333

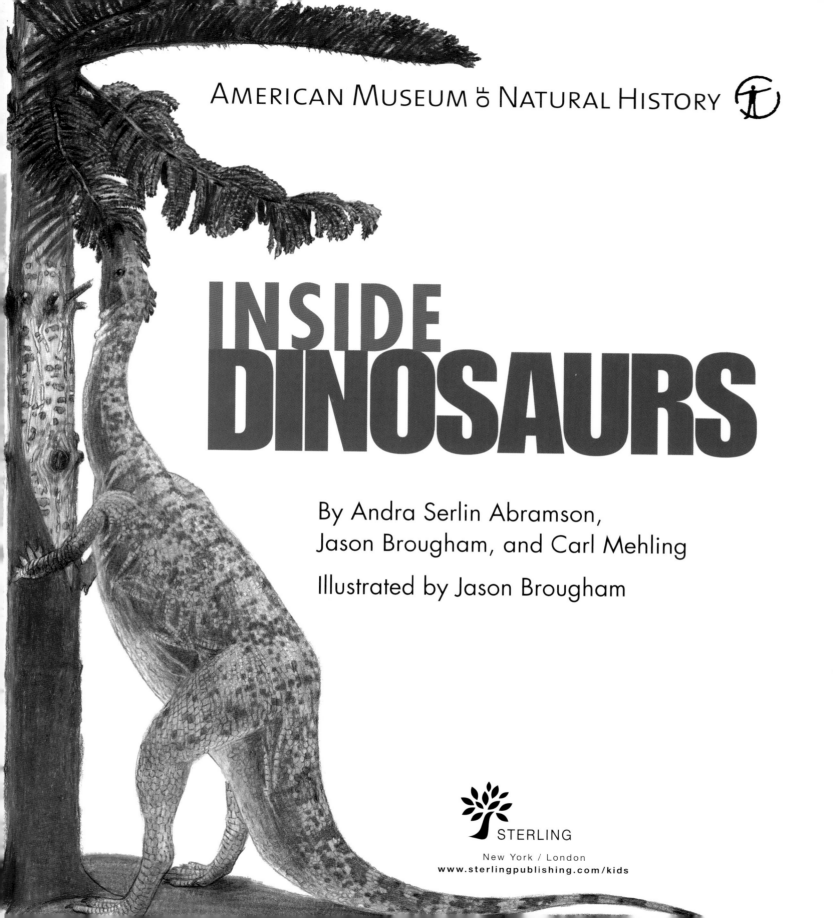

AMERICAN MUSEUM ᵒₕ NATURAL HISTORY

INSIDE
DINOSAURS

By Andra Serlin Abramson,
Jason Brougham, and Carl Mehling

Illustrated by Jason Brougham

STERLING

New York / London
www.sterlingpublishing.com/kids

STERLING and the distinctive Sterling logo are
registered trademarks of Sterling Publishing Co., Inc.

Library of Congress Cataloging-in-Publication Data Available

2 4 6 8 10 9 7 5 3 1
05/10

Published by Sterling Publishing Co., Inc.
387 Park Avenue South, New York, NY 10016
© 2010 by Sterling Publishing Co., Inc.
Illustrations © Jason Brougham
All images courtesy of the American Museum of Natural History except:
Images on pages 6, 8, and 11 are courtesy of Mark Norell.
Images on pages 5, 6 (Roy Chapman Andrews), and 7 are courtesy of Istock.com.

Cover Illustration by Jason Brougham

Distributed in Canada by Sterling Publishing
c/o Canadian Manda Group, 165 Dufferin Street
Toronto, Ontario, Canada M6K 3H6
Distributed in the United Kingdom by GMC Distribution Services
Castle Place, 166 High Street, Lewes, East Sussex, England BN7 1XU
Distributed in Australia by Capricorn Link (Australia) Pty. Ltd.
P.O. Box 704, Windsor, NSW 2756, Australia

Design by Ye Huang & Han Xu

Sterling ISBN 978-1-4027-7074-6 (hardcover)
ISBN 978-1-4027-7778-3 (paperback)

For information about custom editions, special sales, premium and
corporate purchases, please contact Sterling Special Sales Department
at 800-805-5489 or specialsales@sterlingpublishing.com.

Contents

Gobi Desert

Straddling Mongolia's southern border with China, the vast and desolate Gobi Desert is a paleontological treasure chest.

A Real-Life Indiana Jones:
Roy Chapman Andrews

You've probably heard of Indiana Jones, but did you know that the famous movie character might actually be based on the life and adventures of a real paleontologist? Roy Chapman Andrews was an explorer for the American Museum of Natural History during the early twentieth century. He is best known for his expeditions to the Gobi Desert in Mongolia. There, he found the first nests of dinosaur eggs ever discovered.

Roy Chapman Andrews

Roy Chapman Andrews collected many specimens of modern animals and fossils throughout his varied career. He also found some new species of dinosaurs and fossils of ancient mammals that coexisted with these dinosaurs.

Meet Some Paleontologists:
Mike Novacek and Mark Norell

Mike Novacek and Mark Norell have jobs most people only dream about. As scientists for the American Museum of Natural History, they travel each year to the Gobi Desert in Mongolia to dig for fossils of ancient animals. Mike specializes in the mammals that lived millions of years ago. He wants to understand how the prehistoric fossils are related to modern mammals—including humans. Mark's passion is figuring out how some dinosaurs evolved into modern birds. Together, Mike and Mark discovered a site called Ukhaa Tolgod, a dinosaur graveyard where hundreds of fossils have been found.

Ukhaa Tolgod Badlands

Badlands, like Ukhaa Tolgod, named for their poor agricultural potential, are often the best type of land to a paleontologist.

Mike Novacek and Mark Norell

Both Mike Novacek and Mark Norell are passionate and experienced fossil collectors and have led the American Museum's Mongolian expeditions for nearly twenty years.

What Is a Paleontologist?

PALEONTOLOGISTS ARE SCIENTISTS WHO ARE TRAINED to study prehistoric animals, plants, fungi, and even microbes to get a better idea of what life on the earth was like millions of years ago. While you may picture paleontologists out in the field digging up dinosaur bones, that's actually only a small part of what these scientists do. A paleontologist may spend a few weeks of the year out on an expedition, but the real work takes place in the lab, where the specimens are studied and classified.

The Earliest Dinosaur Hunters

Paleontology might seem like a modern scientific study, but people have been finding and studying fossils since the earliest recorded history. The great engineer and artist Leonardo da Vinci studied fossils during the fifteenth century. Georges Cuvier, known as the "father of paleontology," lived during the eighteenth century. He was the first scientist to determine that animal species had become extinct in the past. The term **dinosaur** was created by Richard Owen in 1842. During the late nineteenth and early twentieth centuries, large-scale dinosaur fossils began to be unearthed and reconstructed. From these discoveries grew the modern field of dinosaur paleontology.

Did You Know?

Paleontology belongs to a branch of geology known as historical geology, or the study of Earth's physical history.

Georges Cuvier

The French comparative anatomist and paleontologist Georges Cuvier was the most influential naturalist of the early nineteenth-century. In addition, he was the most important figure in establishing the theory of extinction.

Richard Owen

Famed for coining the word "Dinosauria" in 1842, English biologist Richard Owen was opposed to the theory of evolution by natural selection as described by Charles Darwin.

Looking Through
a Paleontologist's Ey

MILLIONS OF YEARS AGO, WAY BEFORE H
walked the earth, dinosaurs lived on the land and flew thr
sky. Today, paleontologists walk in the steps of ancient d
searching for clues that will tell us more about these magnificent

Struthiomimus

Euoplocephalus

Modern paleontologists are still discovering amazing things and finding innovative ways to extract new information from old bones.

Let's learn to look through a paleontologist's eyes and take a trip back to the time when fierce *Albertosaurus* stalked prey in the forests, spike-frilled *Styracosaurus* grazed in the ferns, groups of *Corythosaurus* hung out, and early birds darted through the sky. Join us as we explore the world of the dinosaur to get an inside look at the lives of these amazing creatures from long ago.

Word Power!

Paleo = really old
Ology = the study of
Paleontology = the study
of ancient living things

A Day in the Life of a Paleontologist

On a typical day of a dig, team members spend the morning searching for fossils. It is not unusual for expedition members to spend hours staring at the ground. Knowing what to look for takes practice and experience. In the afternoon, paleontologists work to preserve the fossils they've found that morning and get them back to camp before the sun goes down. Once night falls, the paleontologists and their team cook dinner and get ready for another night under the stars. There aren't many luxuries on a dig, but for paleontologists, there's nowhere else they'd rather be.

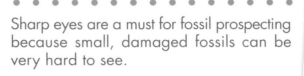

Sharp eyes are a must for fossil prospecting because small, damaged fossils can be very hard to see.

Planning a Dig

Planning a dig starts many months before the actual digging begins. Most dinosaur dig sites are in the most remote places on Earth. That means there are no stores for the scientists to buy anything they might need. Instead, they have to first ship everything to the site by cargo ship and then by truck, which can take several weeks. Outfitting an expedition costs a lot of money and takes a lot of time. Since the team never knows exactly what they will encounter, they try to plan ahead for all emergencies, from a broken down truck to a broken arm.

Patience and tolerance are essential when finding and extracting fossils due to the wide range of environmental conditions.

Since fossils are often found in rock, and rock tends to be heavy, physical strength is always helpful on paleontological expeditions.

A convoy of trucks is used to bring all the materials and supplies needed for a dig.

Tools of the Paleontologist

Some of the tools paleontologists use to uncover fossils hidden for millions of years haven't changed much over the last two hundred years. Shovels, picks, and chisels are still the primary tools needed on a dig, and a simple compass might be used to help scientists find their way. But that doesn't mean paleontology is stuck in the Dark Ages. Today's scientists use Global Positioning Systems (GPS) to locate new places to dig. Back at the lab, computers are used to examine fossils and classify them. Electron microscopes, DNA testing, and computerized axial tomography (CAT) equipment have also become important in helping researchers make great strides in learning more about these ancient animals.

Although many dinosaur fossils are enormous, a microscope is needed to look closely at the many details from the huge specimens and to understand ancient ecosystems better.

Various common tools have been and are still being used to collect fossils.

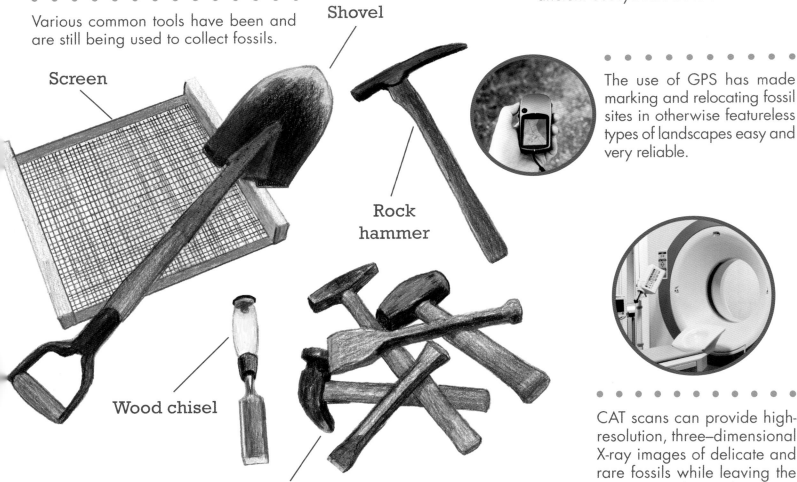

Shovel

Screen

Rock hammer

Wood chisel

Mallet, hammers, and cold chisels

The use of GPS has made marking and relocating fossil sites in otherwise featureless types of landscapes easy and very reliable.

CAT scans can provide high-resolution, three–dimensional X-ray images of delicate and rare fossils while leaving the specimen unharmed.

Dinosaur Places

FOR MOST OF THEIR TIME ON EARTH, DINOSAURS HAVE lived all over the world. Dinosaur fossils, however, have only been found in certain places. The locations shown on this world map are hotspots where fossils such as bones, footprints, and eggs of lots of different dinosaurs have been found. Paleontologists return to these same dig sites over and over again. Each year, previously undiscovered fossils could possibly be exposed by erosion, windstorms, or just plain luck.

United States

The western United States was the very first place where many full skeletons of fossil dinosaurs were found. This abundance is still to be found in deposits that regularly supply paleontologists with well-preserved specimens. Famous sites include the Late Triassic Ghost Ranch Quarries of New Mexico, the Late Jurassic Bone Cabin Quarry of Wyoming (pictured), and the vast Hell Creek Formation.

United Kingdom

The first non-avian dinosaurs to be recognized by science were found in England and described in the 1820s and '30s. Dinosaurs outside of birds are referred to as non-avian dinosaurs. Dinosaur fossil finds are rare in the UK, but they have been very important to the development of Paleontology These include *Megalosaurus*, *Iguanodon*, and *Hylaeosaurus*. To this day, dinosaurs are regularly found in places like the Isle of Wight and Oxfordshire. Pictured here is a dinosaur quarry in Surrey, England.

Germany

The limestone quarries of Solnhofen, Germany, (pictured) have been the source of all of the known specimens of *Archaeopteryx*. This early feathered dinosaur has been an important animal in the discussion of bird origins ever since the first one was found in the mid-1800s. Germany is also duly famous for its vast accumulations of the Late Triassic prosauropod *Plateosaurus*.

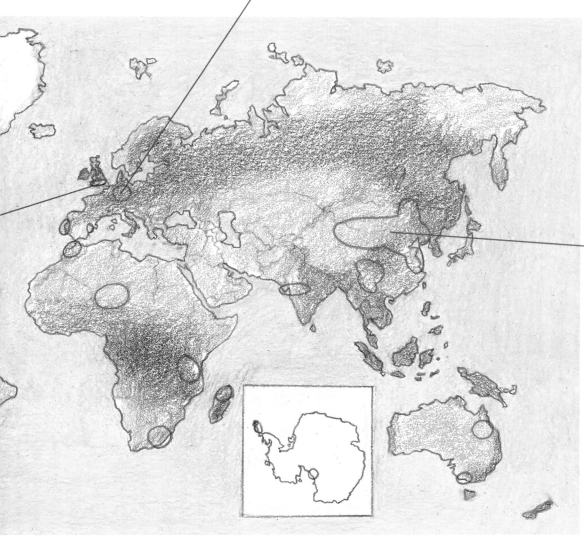

Mongolia

Certain areas of Mongolia and China, especially the Gobi Desert (pictured), are extermely rich in dinosaur fossils, which have been collected by paleontologists since the 1920s. Many famous dinosaurs including *Protoceratops*, *Oviraptor*, *Velociraptor*, *Microraptor*, and *Anchiornis* are known only from these deposits. But Mongolia is probably best known for its abundant non-avian dinosaur eggs.

Tail probably used as a "third leg" when rearing on its hind limbs

Long neck likely enabled it to
eat leaves off high trees

Plateosaurus

Another early dinosaur was *Plateosaurus*, or
"flat lizard." *Plateosaurus* was a large dinosaur
with a long neck and large body. It is one of
the first known herbivorous, or plant-eating,
dinosaurs and lived around 200 million years
ago. Here, *Plateosaurus* uses its long neck to
browse among the leaves.

The Earliest Dinosaurs

YOU MAY THINK YOU KNOW A DINOSAUR WHEN YOU SEE one, but dinosaurs are probably more varied and wonderful than you realize. Although they vary greatly in size and have vastly different features, all dinosaurs share at least seventeen anatomical characteristics. When scientists study an animal's fossilized bones and find features like a perforated hip socket, an ankle bone with a long blade that extends up the shin, and a bony shelf in the pelvis, they know they've found a dinosaur fossil. All dinosaurs have these, which they inherited from one common ancestor—the first dinosaur that ever existed.

Plaque fossil of *Coelophysis*.

Coelophysis

Coelophysis was one of the first dinosaurs. It lived about 228 million years ago. It was a small meat-eating, two-legged dinosaur. Scientists believe *Coelophysis* was a fast runner. It had a long neck and tail.

Highlighted in orange on the pelvis of *Velociraptor* are two features that all dinosaurs have in common. One is a hole that goes right through the hip sockets. Anatomists call this a *perforate acetabulum*. The other is a shelf behind the hip that is called the *brevis fossa*.

The area highlighted in orange of the ankle bone from *Deinonychus* is called the *astragalus*. This bone runs up the front of the shin and is shared by all dinosaurs.

What Is a Fossil?

Fossils are the remains or traces of ancient life that are usually buried in rocks. Examples include bones, teeth, shells, leaf impressions, nests, and footprints. They are evidence of what life was like long ago. Fossils also show how organisms changed over time and how they are related to one another. Unfortunately, fossils cannot tell us everything. While fossils reveal important information about what ancient living things looked like, they keep us guessing about their color, sounds, and most of their behavior.

Almost all fossils are preserved in sedimentary rocks. These rocks are made of materials like sand, soil, and mud. Sometimes, they contain the remains of organisms such as shells, leaves, or skeletons. These materials are deposited at the mouths of rivers, on the bottom of lakes or lagoons, or in sand dunes, and they build up thick layers over millions of years. Over time, they compress and go through chemical changes, slowly turning into sedimentary rock.

Dinosaur fossils have been found all over the world, often by amateur fossil hunters. However, it usually takes a trained expert to collect a fossil without damaging it and in a way that allows crucial information to be recorded about where and when the ancient animal lived.

Did You Know?

Dinosaurs were just one of many groups of animals that arose and flourished around 228 million years ago. Some other groups included marine reptiles, like icthyosaurs and plesiosaurs, and the first flying vertebrates, such as pterosaurs. Although pterosaurs are sometimes mistakenly referred to as dinosaurs, they do not share the common dinosaur ancestor, and so they are not really dinosaurs.

Late Jurassic Period • 151mya • Colorado, USA

Here, *Allosaurus* guards its kill and rests in the shade on a riverbank. It has killed a *Camptosaurus*, and the carcass has attracted the *Goniopholis*. On the opposite bank, a family of *Diplodocus* heads upriver. Further up, a pair of *Brachiosaurus* has come to find rough stones to swallow (see page 39). *Harpactognathus* is fishing over the river. In the foreground is a small unnamed maniraptoran.

Late Triassic Period • 210mya • Arizona, USA

There is actually only *one* dinosaur in this scene, *Coelophysis,* running along the riverbank in the foreground. These ecosystems were the first that the dinosaurs adapted to. In this scene, a pair of *Placerias* (an early mammal relative) is on the opposite bank, *Eudimorphodon* (a pterosaur) is flying over the river, and *Rutiodon* (a crocodile relative) is basking in the sun.

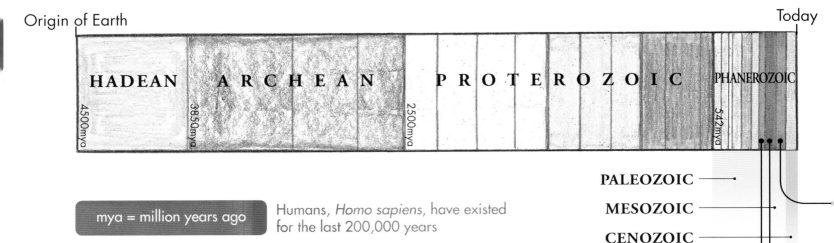

Origin of Earth

Today

| HADEAN | ARCHEAN | PROTEROZOIC | PHANEROZOIC |

4500mya 3850mya 2500mya 542mya

mya = million years ago

Humans, *Homo sapiens*, have existed for the last 200,000 years

PALEOZOIC

MESOZOIC

CENOZOIC

The Age of Dinosaurs

THE HISTORY OF LIFE ON EARTH GOES BACK AT least 3.8 billion years. The "Age of Dinosaurs" represents about 5% of all that length of time. Scientists refer to this as the Mesozoic Era. The Mesozoic was further divided into three sections— the Triassic, Jurassic, and Cretaceous periods—with various smaller subdivisions within each of them.

Different types of dinosaurs lived during the different subdivisions of these periods. You can think of the Triassic as the time when the first dinosaurs were evolving. The Jurassic saw the rise of the giant long-necked sauropods. The Cretaceous was when *Tyrannosaurus* and *Triceratops* lived. Even though the Age of Dinosaurs has passed, one group of dinosaurs survives today—the birds.

Humans, on the other hand, have only been around for about 200 thousand years.

Dinosaur Classification

TO REPRESENT AND CLASSIFY EACH DINOSAUR, RESEARCHERS use a diagram called a cladogram. A cladogram classifies each species based on its evolutionary ancestry, like a family tree. It's a way of organizing dinosaurs based on the unique characteristics they share, like a three-toed foot or a hole in the hip socket. A dinosaur's measurements and hundreds of characteristics are recorded for each species. Then the characteristics are fed into a computer that arranges the animals into cladograms that show the best fit.

Reading a Dinosaur Cladogram

Different clades, or groups, of dinosaurs share similar characteristics. The highest-level taxon (a named group of similar organisms) is Dinosauria, which was created by Richard Owen. All animals in the Dinosauria superorder share a depression forming a hole in the hip socket, a bony shelf on the pelvis, and an ankle bone with a thin blade up the front of the shin, as shown on page 15.

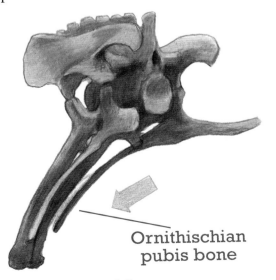

The Dinosauria superorder is then divided into two groups, the Saurischia (lizard-hipped) and Ornithischia (bird-hipped). These two clades are very important, because all dinosaurs, based on their hip structures, are divided into one or the other. The pubis bone (part of the structure of the hip) points downward and to the front in most of the saurischians. In ornithischians, it points downward and toward the tail. Despite the name, it was the "lizard-hipped" dinosaurs that gave rise to modern-day birds, not the "bird-hipped" dinosaurs. The names for the groups were originally given based on their broad similarities rather than on the assumption that the groups were actually related.

Saurischian
pubis bone

Ornithischian
pubis bone

Early Cretaceous Period • 125mya • Liaoning, China

It is a clear day in autumn on the banks of one of the many lakes in this region. The leaves of the ginkgo trees are turning to their fall colors. A pair of *Caudipteryx* feed on fruits from fallen branches. They are spotted by a hunting *Sinornithosaurus*. In the tree branches overhead are, from left to right, a pair of the advanced birds *Liaoningornis*, the mammal *Sinodelphys*, and the bird *Shanweiniao*. Over the lake, *Haopterus* and a flock of the early bird *Confuciusornis* are fishing. Across the lake, we see a herd of *Jinzhousaurus*. On the horizon, the peak of a dormant volcano can be seen.

Late Cretaceous Period • 75mya • Montana, USA

This is an upland forest of conifers and ferns along with new flowering plants, including *Platanus* trees, witch hazel, *Fortunearia*, and low palmettos. *Gorgosaurus*, to the left, is trailing the *Euoplocephalus* and her hatchling calves. A large, unnamed pterosaur is in the sky. *Avisaurus*, with orange markings, is in the pine tree. *Piksi* is the bird skimming over the palmettos. To the right is a small herd of *Maiasaura*.

pterosaur

Avisaurus

Gorgosaurus

Euoplocephalus

Piksi

Maiasaura

Paleobotany

Paleobotany is the study of plants and plant communities of the earth's past. It is a subdiscipline of paleontology. Paleobotanists study fossil plants, like petrified wood, leaf impressions, pollen, amber, and even fossil fruits, seeds, and flowers to get detailed information about the climates and ecology of the different stages of the history of life on Earth.

Age

70.6mya

Late

CRETACEOUS

99.6mya

Early

145.5mya

Late

JURASSIC

161mya

Middle

176mya

Early

201mya

TRIASSIC

Late

235mya

Middle

245mya

Early

Mononykus olecranus

Sauroposeidon proteles

Sinornithoides youngi

Archaeopteryx lithographica

Huayangosaurus taibaii

Eshanosaurus deguchiianus

Eoraptor lunensis

21

Saurischians

The saurischians are made up of the theropods and sauropodomorphs, and their early relatives. The theropods include all of the predatory dinosaurs, like *Coelophysis*, *Ceratosaurus*, and *Tyrannosaurus*, plus all the birds. The sauropodomorphs are made up of all the immense, long-necked, long-tailed herbivores, the largest land animals of all time, like *Apatosaurus*, *Diplodocus*, and *Argentinosaurus*, plus their early relatives, like *Plateosaurus*.

Most theropods had three strong fingers with large, hooked talons for grabbing prey.

Word Power!

Sauro = lizard
Poda = foot
Sauropoda = lizard-footed dinosaur

Ornithischians

The ornithischians are made up of the thyreophorans, ornithopods, and marginocephalians, and their early relatives. Thyreophorans include stegosaurs like *Huayangosaurus* and *Stegosaurus*, and ankylosaurs like *Euoplocephalus* and *Edmontonia*. The ornithopods include all the duckbills, like *Parasaurolophus* and *Edmontosaurus*, and others like *Iguanodon*. The marginocephalians are all the horned dinosaurs and their relatives, like *Protoceratops*, *Psittacosaurus*, and *Torosaurus*, and boneheads like *Pachycephalosaurus*.

Tianyulong

Tianyulong was described in 2009. It is closely related to the ancestor of all ornithischians. The fossil of *Tianyulong* was covered with long, hollow filaments (long, threadlike fibers) that resemble stiff hair or simple feathers.

Sauropod dinosaurs evolved to have extremely long necks and tails. This is one vertebra from the neck of *Apatosaurus*. They also have hollowed out bones to save weight.

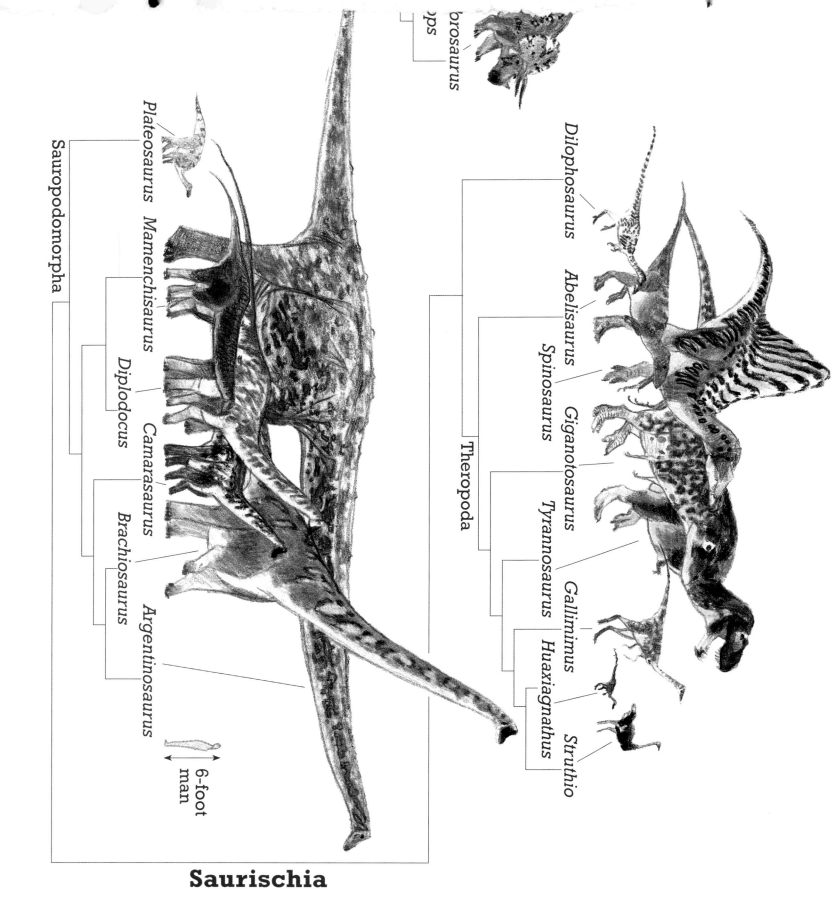

Saurischia

Sauropodomorpha

Plateosaurus

Mamenchisaurus

Diplodocus

Camarasaurus

Brachiosaurus

Argentinosaurus

Theropoda

Dilophosaurus

Abelisaurus

Spinosaurus

Giganotosaurus

Tyrannosaurus

Gallimimus

Huaxiagnathus

Struthio

6-foot man

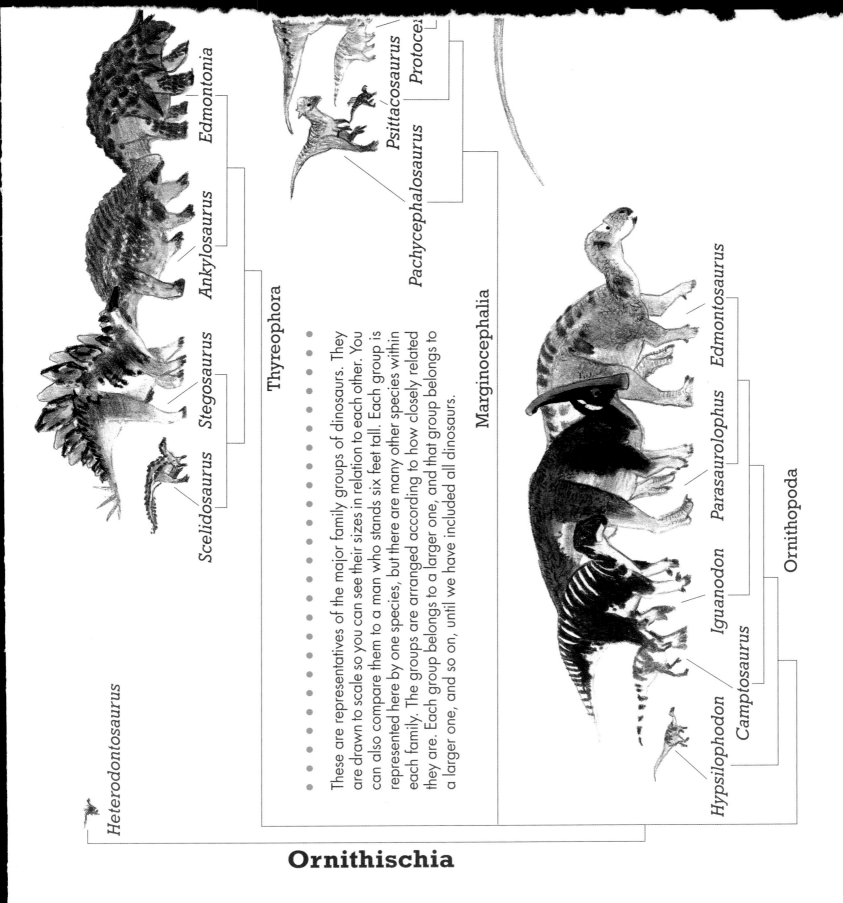

Edmontonia

Psittacosaurus

Protocei

Ankylosaurus

Pachycephalosaurus

Stegosaurus

Thyreophora

Scelidosaurus

Marginocephalia

Edmontosaurus

These are representatives of the major family groups of dinosaurs. They are drawn to scale so you can see their sizes in relation to each other. You can also compare them to a man who stands six feet tall. Each group is represented here by one species, but there are many other species within each family. The groups are arranged according to how closely related they are. Each group belongs to a larger one, and that group belongs to a larger one, and so on, until we have included all dinosaurs.

Parasaurolophus

Iguanodon

Ornithopoda

Camptosaurus

Hypsilophodon

Heterodontosaurus

Ornithischia

Dinosaur Sizes

YOU MAY PICTURE DINOSAURS AS ENORMOUS CREATURES whose every footstep made the earth tremble, and there certainly were dinosaurs that large. However, of the more than 500 known species of non-avian dinosaurs (dinosaurs outside of birds are referred to as non-avian dinosaurs), only a few were as big as a school bus. Many were not any bigger than a large dog, and some were so tiny you could hold them in your hands.

Tyrannosaurus: A Life History

Evidence suggests that *Tyrannosaurus* started out as an egg that weighed only a few pounds and then grew to full size in just over twenty years. In its teens, *Tyrannosaurus* would have been gaining around 4 pounds every single day and about 1,600 pounds a year.

Tyrannosaurus

Tyrannosaurus is arguably the most popular dinosaur, as it possesses many of the characteristics people find most alluring about the tyrannosaurid group: huge size and frightening form.

Did You Know?

One of only a few *Tyrannosaurus* footprints ever found was discovered in Montana in 2007. At amazing 29 inches long, the mark was made by the giant dinosaur as it walked across a prehistoric floodplain more than 65 million years ago.

Just Hatched!

LOOKING AT DIFFERENT TYPES OF FOSSILIZED DINOSAUR nests has provided paleontologists with some great information about non-avian dinosaurs. For example, researchers noticed that different types of dinosaurs arranged their eggs differently within the nest. Also, adults have been found fossilized, still sitting on their eggs, confirming that some non-avian dinosaurs actually sat on their nests, just as modern-day dinosaurs—birds—do today.

Citipati Chicks Hatching

Studies suggest that, like with birds, this clutch of twenty-four eggs was laid by their mother on different days, yet will all hatch on the same day. As with some modern birds, the chicks may have been able to walk and find their own food in just a day or two.

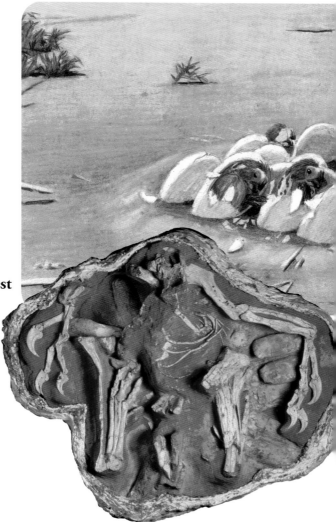

Dinosaur Eggs and Babies

Fragile embryos, hatchlings, and juveniles are some of the rarest fossilized dinosaur specimens. The embryos found in fossilized dinosaur eggs shed light on ancient dinosaur development and sometimes help to identify which type of dinosaur built which type of nest. A few times, paleontologists were lucky enough to uncover fossilized dinosaur nests that had the remains of baby dinosaurs still in them. Hatchlings found in or near nests hint that some non-avian dinosaurs may have nurtured their young, although it is uncertain how long this care was given.

The biggest dinosaur known, Argentinosaurus, stands 16.4 feet tall. Here it is shown walking up Central Park West, right past the main entrance of the American Museum of Natural History.

Anchiornis

The man in front is six feet tall. Perched on his left hand is *Anchiornis*. Hovering over the man's face is *Mellisuga helenae*, the Bee Hummingbird, which is just over two inches long.

The Biggest Dinosaurs

Not all dinosaurs were big, but the biggest ones outweighed anything that ever walked on the earth. One of the largest dinosaurs ever discovered is *Argentinosaurus*, weighing in at a hefty 176,000 pounds. Researchers debate whether these huge dinosaurs were just big, or whether they were fast, too. Some analyses have predicted that the giant predators, like the ones seen in the movie *Jurassic Park*, could have run as fast as a car. However, other research indicates that these animals probably moved slowly, not going much faster than a leisurely walk.

The Smallest Dinosaurs

Since birds are considered by scientists to be part of the dinosaur group, the smallest dinosaur known so far is the Bee Hummingbird, which weighs only about .06 ounces. This tiny bird is about the size of a bee and can be found today in Cuba. The smallest non-avian dinosaur ever discovered is *Anchiornis*. Scientists estimate that *Anchiornis*, found in China just a few years ago, would have weighed only about 3.5 ounces. *Anchiornis* means "close to birds," and it is considered an important link between ancient dinosaurs and modern birds.

Stage 1:

The *Tyrannosaurus* life cycle would begin.

Stage 2:

Scientists expect that a hatchling *Tyrannosaurus* had a body covered in scales and downy feathers that provided insulation and conserved body heat. Fossils show that smaller members of the group had simple downlike or hairlike feathers.

Stage 3:

A two-year-old *Tyrannosaurus* would likely be a nimble and feathered predator. Once it reached a weight of about 300 pounds, the feathers would no longer be needed for insulation and they probably shed from the skin.

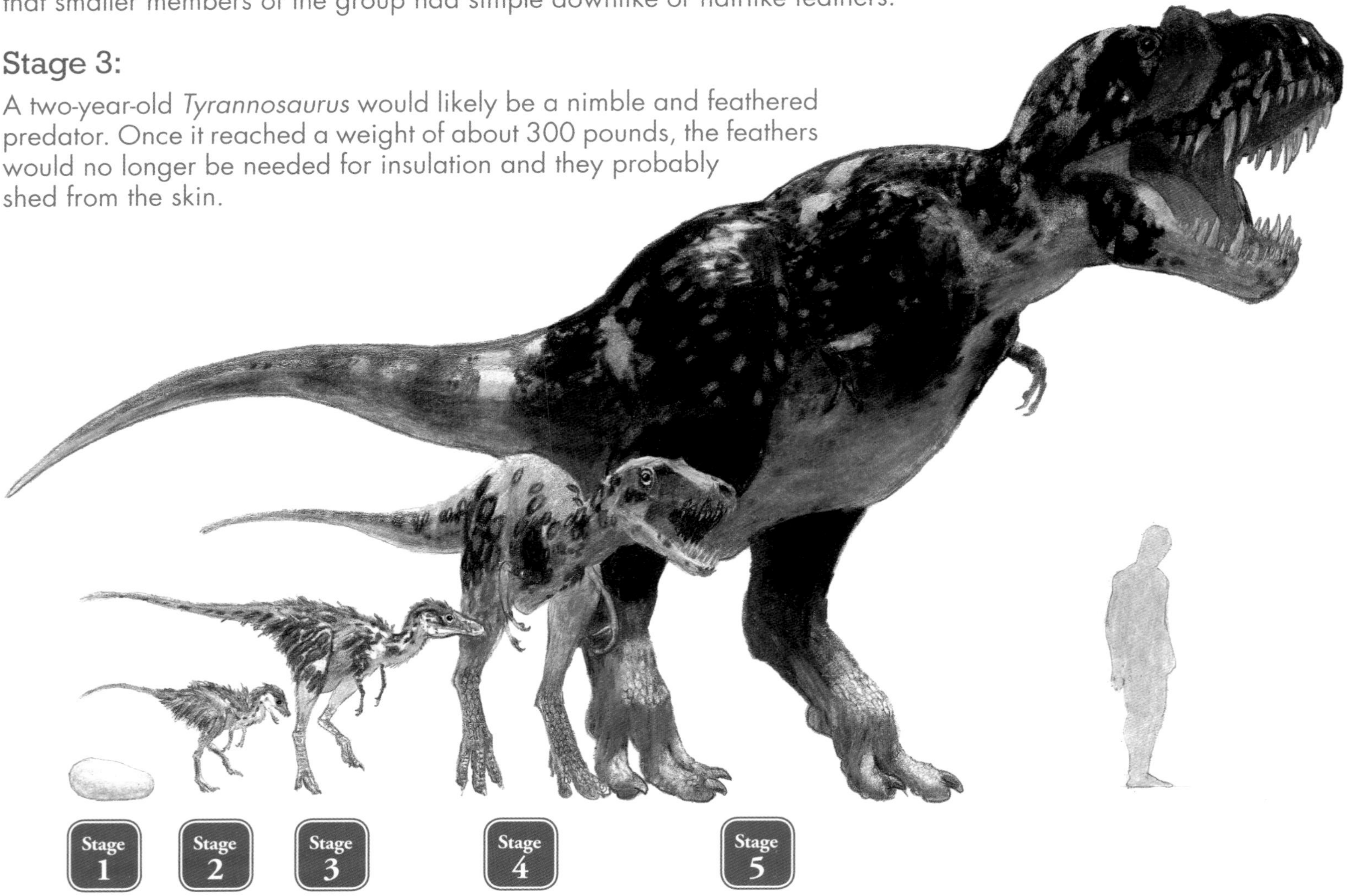

Stage 1   Stage 2   Stage 3   Stage 4   Stage 5

Stage 4:

By the time a *Tyrannosaurus* was eleven years old, it would have weighed about 880 pounds. At this point it would have been growing fast and was still likely able to run fast.

Stage 5:

By 28 years old, the largest and oldest *Tyrannosaurus* would have weighed about 12,345 pounds. It was too big to run very fast. Older *Tyrannosaurus* fossils usually have evidence of broken bones and other injuries.

29

Citipati Father Shading Nest

Oviraptorids nested in the open, in the arid habitat of Cretaceous Mongolia. Here the father *Citipati* is panting in the hot sun and shading his hatchlings until they are strong enough to head into the brush for shade. Birds like the peregrine falcon do this today, and some researchers suggest that wings might have first evolved to help brood eggs and chicks.

Dinosaur Nest Discoveries

Fossilized dinosaur nests discovered at the Ukhaa Tolgod dig site in Mongolia revealed that several types of dinosaurs had laid eggs there. So far, researchers have uncovered five types of fossilized dinosaur eggs varying in shape and size. Another important dinosaur nesting site was found at Auca Mahuevo in the Patagonia province of Argentina. There, paleontologists found hundreds of nests spaced almost equally apart. They also found eggs containing embryonic remains. The large number of eggs gave scientists important information about the nesting and parenting behavior of these ancient creatures. It also gave them clues to the environment in which these dinosaurs lived and nested, the ages of these dinosaurs, and their nesting behavior.

Recreated Citipati Mother and Chicks

This artist's reconstruction of a brooding *Citipati* was created for the American Museum of Natural History. It is based on a pair of extraordinary fossils that preserve the nesting behavior of this large species, which strongly suggests that they were feathered.

Feeding Time

Some theropods were almost certainly hunters. Researchers believe that a dinosaur like _Bambiraptor_ would have chased and caught small lizards, frogs, turtles, fish, pterosaurs, birds, and mammals that lived in its habitat. Predatory dinosaurs would also have been interested in the nests and young of other dinosaurs. Each nest would have thirty or more eggs or small hatchlings, which would have been easy prey if ungaurded. Other dinosaurs may have

primarily been scavengers, which avoided hunting and, instead, foraged for animals that died from illness, injury, drought, or starvation. Both hunters and scavengers needed strong jaws and sharp teeth to tear off great hunks of flesh from their prey, and at least some of them actually swallowed the bones whole.

There are now many fossils in which the dinosaurs' stomach contents were preserved. In other fossils, the teeth of predatory dinosaurs are lodged into the bones of their prey. These fossils reveal some of the things we know for certain that non-avian dinosaurs ate.

When the fossil of this giant pterosaur was found, its tibia (shinbone) had _Saurornitholestes_ teeth embedded in it. The pterosaur was so large that the dinosaur likely scavenged it after it was already dead.

Did You Know?

Only a few non-avian dinosaurs are thought to be omnivores, which means they ate both plants and animals. Some examples of omnivores are _Ornithomimus_, _Troodon_, and _Oviraptor_. These dinosaurs probably ate mixed diets of foods such as plants, eggs, insects, and meat.

Meat-eating Teeth

Most non-avian theropods had sharp, curved, and serrated teeth designed to slice easily through animal tissue.
Like crocodiles and sharks today, the teeth were shed throughout the animal's life and new ones grew in as replacements. The number of teeth each dinosaur had varied widely. Researchers believe *Tyrannosaurus* had fifty to sixty teeth, some as large as 13 inches long, including the root. *Velociraptor* had about eighty teeth and *Baryonyx* had nearly one hundred, with sixty-four teeth in its lower jaw and thirty-two in the upper.

Ceratosaurus was a large predator of the Late Jurassic Period. It has the bladelike, serrated teeth that were characteristic of carnivorous dinosaurs.

Theropod Teeth

Theropod teeth have tiny denticles on the cutting edges, which make them sharp, like a shark tooth. Denticles allowed theropods to slice through tough hide, sinew, and muscle. They also made it possible for them to obtain a lot of nourishment from tough carcasses. When magnified, these denticles look like the teeth on a saw.

The Meat Eaters: Carnivores

SHARP, CURVED TALONS, SERRATED TEETH, STRONG RUNNING legs, and keen eyesight are common features in most types of theropods, and this marks them as predators. But just like eagles or alligators do today, most predators will also eat animals they find that are already dead, making it harder for scientists to be sure if predatory dinosaurs worked together in groups when hunting.

Deinonychus vs. Tenontosaurus

Tenontosaurus was a 2,000 pound herbivore. *Deinonychus* was a wolf-size carnivorous dinosaur that lived in the same habitat. There are fossil sites that preserve multiple specimens of the two species together. Some of the *Tenontosaurus* bones even show tooth scratches from *Deinonychus* teeth, and have shed teeth lying among them. Some researchers suggest this is evidence of a *Deinonychus* pack attacking a *Tenontosaurus* herd, while other studies indicate that because *Deinonychus* bones were also bitten, it may have been a scavenging site.

This scene is inspired by fossil findings from the Antlers Formation in southeastern Oklahoma. It depicts four *Deinonychus* pursuing a juvenile *Tenontosaurus* on a dry floodplain in southeast Oklahoma about 109 million years ago.

In the exhibit "Fighting Dinosaurs," the American Museum of Natural History re-created a scene from 80 million years ago in which a *Protoceratops* prepares to face off against *Velociraptor*. The fossil for which the exhibit was named shows these two dinosaurs locked in combat just as they were found in Mongolia.

A reconstructed close-up of *Protoceratops* from the "Fighting Dinosaurs" exhibit.

This incredible model preserves a fight between the carnivorous *Velociraptor*, on the right, and the herbivorous *Protoceratops*, on the left.

The "Fighting Dinosaurs"

Paleontologists excavated fossils of two dinosaurs apparently locked in combat. They were buried in a landslide while they were fighting, and were preserved in this action pose after 80 million years. *Velociraptor* was a fierce carnivore that hunted prey, such as the plant-eating *Protoceratops*. Here, the *Velociraptor* has embedded its deadly foot claw into the neck of the crouching *Protoceratops*. In turn, the *Protoceratops* appears to have bitten and broken the right arm of the *Velociraptor*. The specimen was discovered in 1971 and is considered a national treasure of Mongolia.

Velociraptor and *Protoceratops* fossils locked in battle.

Coelophysis was found with bones in its stomach. For decades it was thought it had cannibalized its own young. Re-examination showed that the bones belonged to a small crocodylomorph, probably Hesperosuchus.

Confuciusornis was found with vertebrae and ribs from the small fish Jinanichthys in its throat.

Baryonyx was found with the scales of the large fish Lepidotes in its stomach.

One specimen of Sinosauropteryx was found with a whole lizard in its stomach.

Sinocalliopteryx was found with the entire lower leg of a small dromaeosaurid in its stomach. Some small dromaeosaurids had long feathers on their legs.

The Plant Eaters: Herbivores

YOU MAY BE SURPRISED TO DISCOVER THAT WHEN PLANT-eating dinosaurs like *Apatosaurus* looked around for a meal, they were looking at many of the same types of plants found on Earth today. Pine trees and other conifers, ferns, horsetails, and cycads were all found during the time of the non-avian dinosaurs. Researchers have even cut open coprolites—fossilized dinosaur poop—and found chewed up leaves, wood, and seeds from cycads, ferns, and conifer trees.

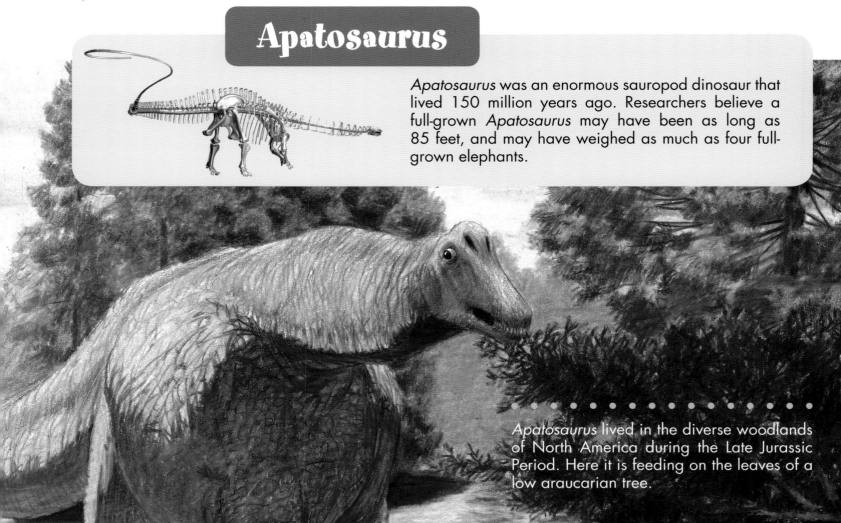

Apatosaurus

Apatosaurus was an enormous sauropod dinosaur that lived 150 million years ago. Researchers believe a full-grown *Apatosaurus* may have been as long as 85 feet, and may have weighed as much as four full-grown elephants.

Apatosaurus lived in the diverse woodlands of North America during the Late Jurassic Period. Here it is feeding on the leaves of a low araucarian tree.

Plant-eater Teeth

Some non-avian plant-eating dinosaurs had peglike or spoon-shaped teeth used for pinching off foliage but not really for chewing. Instead, the tough plant matter was digested in the animal's stomach, possibly aided by gizzard stones, an adaptation of plant-eating animals found in birds today. Gizzard stones are rocks swallowed by the animal. These rocks stay in the stomach, and they are squeezed together by the gizzard muscles, acting like teeth to grind up the plant fiber. When the rocks get worn too smooth, they are regurgitated and new rough ones are swallowed.

Sticking Their Necks Out

The long necks and even longer tails of the huge plant-eating dinosaurs called sauropods are features that puzzle researchers. While scientists are still debating what functions were most likely, highly accurate computer simulations of dinosaur motion have some scientists believing it was impossible for sauropods to hold their necks up like giraffes do. These researchers believe sauropods held their necks parallel to the ground, or angled slightly downward, and then swung their heads back and forth while browsing.

Even though the sauropods may not have been able to reach as high as scientists once thought, their long necks would have allowed them to reach at least twelve feet up into the trees (as seen on pages 13–14 of *Plateosaurus* eating leaves). Some experts believe the huge plant eaters may sometimes have stood on the edges of lakes and swamps, grazing on vegetation growing in shallow water. If they did, their long necks were one way to keep their huge bodies on higher and firmer ground.

The ankylosaur *Minmi* was found with cleanly cut plant tissues includ-ing leaves, possible fern spores, seeds, and possible fruiting bodies in its stomach. Here it is depicted browsing on cycadeoids.

Jeholornis was found with many conifer seeds, maybe pine nuts, in its stomach.

Apatosaurus

Apatosaurus had a rake-like tooth row that helped it to gather conifer needles in bulk, but not to chew.

Dinosaurs of the Air

ALL BIRDS ARE DINOSAURS, BUT IT CAN BE HARD TO TELL where to draw the line between birds and non-avian dinosaurs. Here are features that birds and their closest non-avian relatives share: wing feathers, a wishbone, thin shoulder blades, light hollow bones, a large breastbone, and a foot with three main toes and one smaller one.

The Tails

From left to right are the tail skeletons of *Gallus* (rooster), *Zhongornis* (ancient bird), and *Bambiraptor* (non-avian theropod). *Bambiraptor* has more than twenty-two vertebrae. *Zhongornis* has only thirteen, the last four of which have lateral flanges that were starting to fuse. *Gallus* has only five free vertebrae; the ones on the end are fused together into a pygostyle, which is where the tail feathers of the rooster attach.

Feathers

Fossils prove that *Velociraptor* and other theropod dinosaurs had feathers or featherlike coverings on their bodies. *Caudipteryx*, found in China, is an oviraptorid and it was fully feathered. It had downy feathers on its body, long, flat-vaned feathers on its arms, and a fan of tail feathers. *Sinornithosaurus*, also from China, had these wing-feathers and a body covering of hairlike feathers.

Gallus

40

Different Kinds of Feathers

Once it was possible to define all "animals with feathers" as birds. Now there are fossils of twenty-three types of non-avian dinosaurs that are also "animals with feathers."

The simplest type of feather is drawn here on the far right. It is a down feather. It has many strands that join together at the base and all grow from one follicle. On the left is a similar feather found in fossils of theropod dinosaurs. Tyrannosaurid, compsognathid, and maniraptoran dinosaurs all have them.

Bambiraptor

The next type of feather is on the far right. It is a feather with a quill in the center and vanes of filaments on each side. To the left is a similar type of feather from dromaeo-saurs and oviraptorosaurs.

This is the most evolved type of feather. It has a strong quill and the two vanes are different widths. This type of feather will produce lift in a bird's wing. It is known from dromaeosaurs and birds.

Zhongornis

The Shoulder and Chest

Gallus, *Zhongornis*, and *Bambiraptor* all have a wishbone (called the *furcula*) at the base of their throats. This bone is unique to dinosaurs. In *Bambiraptor* (top), the coracoid is round, but there is a short stalk that elongates it. In *Zhongornis* (middle), the stalk is much longer and the coracoid is much less round. In *Gallus* (bottom), the coracoid is just a long stalk. *Gallus* is different from the other two because it has a deep, triangular keel on its sternum, or breastbone.

41

The Extinction Event

THERE ARE DIFFERENT LINES OF EVIDENCE REGARDING the mass extinction 65 million years ago. Some fossils suggest a gradual decline in the dinosaurs, while others show a sudden catastrophe. Some indicate an asteroid impact or massive volcanic eruptions. These differing possibilities have led to healthy and rigorous scientific debates. However, there is little doubt that all species of non-avian dinosaurs became extinct.

Here a small pod of *Alamosaurus* have survived the asteroid impact in a sheltered valley. Venturing forth, they find that their forest habitat has been flattened by the blast wave and blanketed in a ghostly layer of ash and pulverized rock.

The End Cretaceous Extinction Event

About 65 million years ago, an asteroid or comet hit the earth. It struck the ocean just off what is now the coast of Yucatan, Mexico, near the town of Chicxulub. Although this event is not necessarily the only reason for the extinction, it certainly did devastate the global ecosystem. Many plant and animal species survived the event. Fossil spores from that time show that ferns spread rapidly after the disaster.

A small bird is preparing to feed on new fern shoots that are growing up through the ash. Over millions of years, this bird's offspring will evolve into some of the species of birds that we know today.

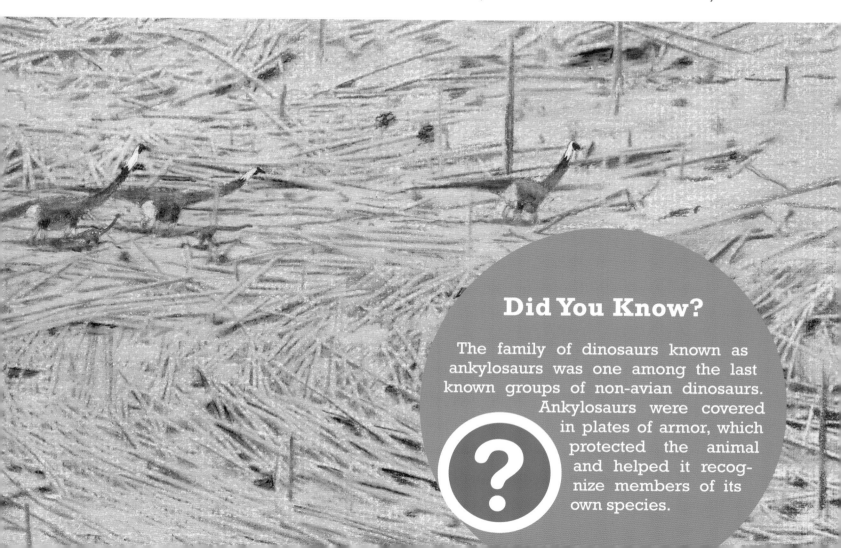

Did You Know?

The family of dinosaurs known as ankylosaurs was one among the last known groups of non-avian dinosaurs. Ankylosaurs were covered in plates of armor, which protected the animal and helped it recognize members of its own species.

How Things Change

EVEN THOUGH PALEONTOLOGISTS NOW KNOW A LOT about dinosaurs and the world they lived in, that doesn't mean they know everything. As newer and better research techniques and equipment develop, scientists sometimes change their minds about how ancient animals lived or worked.

Did You Know?

Scientists refine their understanding as better evidence becomes available. *Velociraptor* was once assumed to be covered with only scaly skin. A new fossil from Mongolia shows attachments for feather ligaments on the arm bone. This is reflected in current restorations that actually show *Velociraptor* with wing feathers.

?

Velociraptor

Here is *Velociraptor* the way it used to be depicted—with scaly skin like a lizard.

Dinosaurs in Your Backyard

The discovery of new dinosaur fossils can happen almost anywhere and at any time. Amateur dinosaur hunters have discovered many fossils and even whole new species. The bones of the dinosaur *Bambiraptor* were found by a fourteen-year-old boy on his family's ranch in Montana. So if you have exposed sedimentary rock in your backyard, don't be afraid to get out there and try to make your very own dinosaur discovery. Don't have any sedimentary rock nearby? Look at the trees…the birds you see are your very own dinosaur discoveries.

Velociraptor

This is *Velociraptor* with feathers. *Velociraptor* lived in an arid habitat, so it is shown here with colors like those of ground birds from desert habitats around the world.

The Hall of Saurischians boasts the world's first exhibited *Tyrannosaurus* skeleton (mounted) in 1915).

Visit the Museum

TO SEE ANCIENT FOSSILS, BONES, AND ARTIFACTS, AND TO get a glimpse of amazing life-size, dinosaur skeletons, you should visit a museum. The American Museum of Natural History in New York City is one of the premier places to learn about prehistoric creatures. While this book can give you a few of the highlights of the museum's collection, only a trip to the actual museum itself will show you just how much there is to see and learn.

This is an animatronic scale model of *Tyrannosaurus* by Hall Train Studios.

Biomechanics

Scientists have been able to answer a lot of questions about non-avian dinosaurs, but exactly how they walked has been debated for nearly 200 years. The answer to questions like this one are coming from an area of science called biomechanics. This approach applies principles of physics and engineering to biological movement. It lets scientists study animals as if they were machines. Experts examine fossils, observe movement in living species, and analyze muscle in order to better understand these ancient giants. Thanks in part to biomechanics, paleontologists can now bring ancient dinosaurs to life!

The Future of Paleontology

HIGH TECHNOLOGY IS COMING INTO PLAY IN SEVERAL ways to help us expand our understanding of dinosaurs. Imaging technologies like CAT scans are extracting better, and even hidden, information from the fossils we have. Molecular biology is turning up astounding new results about the protein sequences of non-avian dinosaurs. The new discovery that some dinosaur molecules have endured over 70 million years inside fossils opens new realms of potential investigation. By modeling fossilized dinosaur bones into computer simulations and comparing them carefully with living animals, sound conclusions can be drawn about the physical capabilities of extinct dinosaurs.

Words To Know

Carnivorous: Meat-eating.

Clade: A group of organisms classified together on the basis of similar features traced back to a common ancestor.

Cladogram: A tree-like diagram that depicts the evolutionary history of a group of organisms. Branching points are where new, advanced features appeared and species diverged from common ancestors.

Denticles: Serrations or tiny toothlike projections.

Evolution: Changes in the genetic composition of a population over time that are passed on from ancestors to subsequent generations.

Extinction: The death of every member of a group of organisms.

Fossil: Any evidence of an organism of a past geologic age, such as a skeleton or leaf imprint.

Fossilized: Converted into a fossil; often when organic substance has been replaced with mineral substances in the remains of an organism.

Fossil record: A term used by paleontologists to refer to the total number of fossils that have been discovered, as well as to the information derived from them.

Furcula: A wishbone; the bone at the base of the throat in birds and other dinosaurs.

Habitat: The area or environment where an organism or ecological community normally lives or occurs.

Herbivorous: Plant-eating.

Extinction Event: A large-scale mass extinction that occurred approximately 65.5 million years ago.

Non-avian dinosaurs: Since most people studying dinosaurs consider birds to be dinosaurs, when scientists now refer to dinosaurs, birds are included, therefore dinosaurs outside of birds are referred to as non-avian dinosaurs.

Paleobotany: The branch of paleontology that deals with plant fossils.

Paleontology: The study of prehistoric life, as represented by the fossils of plants, animals, and other organisms.

Predator: An organism that lives by hunting and eating other organisms.

Pygostyle: The bone at the posterior end of the spinal column in birds and some other dinosaurs, formed by the fusion of several caudal vertebrae.

Bibliography

Burnie, David. *The Concise Dinosaur.* Kingfisher: New York, 2004.

Dixon, Dougal. *Visual Encyclopedia of Dinosaurs.* Dorling Kindersley: New York, 2005.

Norman, David. *Dinosaur.* Dorling Kindersley: New York, 2004.

Weishampel, David B., Peter Dodson, and Halszka Osmólska, eds. *The Dinosauria 2nd edition.* University of California Press, 2004.

http://www.geosociety.org/science/timescale/

Find Out More

Websites:

American Museum of Natural History:

http://www.amnh.org/

http://www.amnh.org/science/

http://www.amnh.org/science/divisions/paleo/

http://www.amnh.org/exhibitions/permanent/fossilhalls/

http://www.amnh.org/ology/

http://www.amnh.org/ology/paleontology/

Books:

Aliki. *Digging Up Dinosaurs.* Harper & Row, Publishers: New York, 1988.

Benton, Michael. *Dinosaur and Other Prehistoric Animal Fact Finder.* Kingfisher: New York, 1992.

Dingus, Lowell and Luis Chiappe. *The Tiniest Giants: Discovering Dinosaur Eggs.* Doubleday: New York, 1999.

Lambert, David. *The Ultimate Dinosaur Book.* Dorling Kindersley: New York, 1993.

Norell, Mark, Eugene Gaffney, and Lowell Dingus. *Discovering Dinosaurs in the American Museum of Natural History.* Alfred A. Knopf: New York, 1995.

Norell, Mark, and Lowell Dingus. *The Nest of Dinosaurs: The Story of Oviraptor.* Doubleday: New York, 1999.

Index